DANTE'S
INFERNAL
PUZZLE
COLLECTION

Published in 2013 by Carlton Books
An imprint of the Carlton Publishing Group
20 Mortimer Street
London W1T 3JW

Copyright © 2013 Carlton Books Limited

A CIP catalogue record for this book is available
from the British Library.

ISBN 978 1 78097 418 7

Printed and bound in Great Britain by CPI Group (UK) Ltd,
Croydon CR0 4YY

DANTE'S
INFERNAL
PUZZLE
COLLECTION

100 hellishly difficult riddles,
cryptic conundrums and merciless enigmas

Tim Dedopulos

CARLTON
BOOKS

All Hope Abandon,

Ye Who Enter Here

You hold within your hands an open tome,
a record of my horrible travails
within that place from where all hope is gone.

My piety was tested there, in Hell,
and likewise so my ingenuity.
Dear friend, for you I reproduce my trials.

Poor Virgil banished, I must be your guide,
and you will take my role as Dante now.
The irony of this is keen to me.

I would say welcome to you now, my friend,
but not in this place, not in this odd way.
Instead, I say good luck and, friend... Be strong.

The Dark Wood Of Error

1. FONTANA

Midway upon the journey of our life, I found myself within a forest dark, for I had lost the path that does not stray.

That forest savage, rough and stern, gave me to think upon a problem old to me. Tartaglia, the stammerer – a fiend, or at the least possessed of a fiend's mind – once posed a riddle vexatious to me. "One fourth of twenty, if it comes to four, then show me what is a third part of ten?"

Dear friend, pray tell me, can you pass this trial?

2. SACCHETTO

This even in mere thought renews my fear: within the forest I was sore beset, by beasts, each filled with deadliness and spite. A panther covered with a spotted skin, a lion fierce with hunger ravenous, and last a she-wolf, lean and meanly made. They thrust me back, denying me my path, and so I wandered lost and free of hope. In my confusion I was driven back, to find all my possessions disarrayed.

Three sacks had I, each one's contents unique. Now, they were labelled, but in all my haste, these labels had in some way been misplaced, and none of them revealed contents true. To find the real content of each sack, when under pressure from such dreadful foes, how few investigations may I make?

3. VIRGIL

When I was rushing down to lower ground, before mine
eyes did one present himself, one who seemed faint, and
then with him another. "Have pity on me," unto him I cried.
"Whichever you may be, if shade or man."

"Not man," said one. "Once man I was. The same, I think,
was true of this one here with me. Be wise, for we are by
compulsion bound, to answer queries in a certain way.
One may speak only truth, the other lies."

The second gave his grave assent to this. I turned to him
and fixed him with my eye. "So which are you?" I asked.
"The truthful one?"

"He'll tell you 'Yes,'" the first of them replied. Which of
the pair was worthy of my trust?

The Descent

4. SEGARE

Day was now departing, and the embrowned air released
the men and animals of earth from their fatigues, and I
myself prepared to journey to the deathless world, with
my poetic spirit guide, Virgil.

Our preparations for descent involved two stages, gathering
and packing up. An hour of gathering would yield five
heaps, the same of packing would have processed eight.
To fill an hour exact, pray tell me then – how many heaps
should we have gathered up?

5. RETAGGIO

O Muses, O High Genius, now assist; O memory that didst write down what I saw, here shall your excellence be manifest. And I began, "Poet, who are my guide, regard my wit, if it be sufficient, ere to that rugged pass you confine me."

"You fear that flood where ocean has no sway? One such as you should be afraid of naught. Take heart; your mind is keen and your wit quick. See here: my cousin had two sons on death, and left to them one hundred florins clear. Were you to take a third of that bequest as given to the younger one, that sum, subtracted from one fourth the elder's gain, would yield eleven coins, no more, no less. So tell me, what did each of them receive?"

6. FEDELTA

"Be strong," my guide commanded me, "and bold. Not
all unlooked-for summonses end in pain. As sweet Lucia
wished, I came to you: I have delivered you from those wild
beasts which barred the lovely mountain's short ascent. In
life, in sooth, I knew a man of means, most jealous of his
tender wife's regard. A warning he received of his dear
love, at home in bed with one unknown to him. He raced to
see,
and found to his surprise, a stranger there entwined
within her arms. And yet was he unmoved to rage or bile,
but overcome with feelings far less stern. Can you reveal
the truth of this event?"

15

The Vestibule Of Hell

7. PREDATORE

A darkness seized me as I read those words. Here sighs, complaints and ululations loud resounded through that night without a star, so that, at this beginning, did I weep. Within, a pair of creatures were in chase, and dashed straight past my startled guide and me. The first, some horrid fowl, had better speed; the latter, born from wolf or dog, more strength.

I reckoned that the fowl was in the lead, by just ten feet and not a whisker more. It ran at speeds of twenty leagues an hour, but I could see it slow, and it was clear, that speed would drop a league each quarter-minute. The hound-thing kept a pace that stayed in true, twelve leagues an hour without any change. It would not deviate from its set course, but just five minutes could it stay the chase. I wonder, did it catch its prey at all?

Through me the way is
to the suffering city...

Through me the way is
to eternal pain...

Through me the way
among the people lost...

All hope abandon,
ye who enter here.

18

8. AGGRUPPAMENTO

So I, who had my head with horror bound, said "Master, what is this which now I hear? What folk are these, so vanquished by their pain?"

And he returned, "This miserable place maintains the sorry souls of those who now mingle here with caitiff angels – not rebel nor faithful, those who stood for self. They have no longer hope in life or death, all other fates denied them for all time."

These miscreants, who never truly lived, were naked and were stung repeatedly by gadflies and by hornets dark and mean. Their blood and tears fell upon their feet, to be gathered up by vile worms.

"A thousand can you see," declared my guide, "within this line before us here, that is. For reasons that are not revealed to me yet, these wretches are arranged in just ten packs, so should a number of them be called out – any sum of them from one to all – one or more whole packs may venture forth, and doing so complete that number called."

"So if I called three hundred..." I began.

"Then four packs would fulfil you that amount. What number do your think each pack contains?"

9. CHARON

Looking far, I saw a great river's bank, and I refrained from speech until its side. And there, towards us headed, in a boat, an ancient man with hair bleached white by time was shouting: "Woe to you, ye souls depraved! I come to lead you to the other shore, to the eternal gloom, in fire and frost."

"Our boatman," said my guide, "is Charon called. He is the pilot of the livid fen. This wretched shore greets all who feared not God. And yet the wicked here are driven on, compelled to venture deeper into Hell, that they may reap the crops that their life sowed."

Three sisters did I spy, entwined in pride, so each did try to prove herself the best, and in so doing prove her lack of heart. In weaving did their competition lie.

"Am I not best?" the youngest cried. "Five shirts I made while Carla made but two."

"Oh, Anna," one replied, "that may be so, but while you crafted three our Maria managed without fail to turn out four. One of your shirts took five times the cloth as one of hers, and three of hers as much as five of mine. So let it be."

Said Anna, "Quiet, Carla; still your whine. Your shirts may have possessed four times the warmth of poor Maria's but mine were warmer still, three times the warmth of yours – no word a lie. For speed and thrift and warmth I am the best."

So she declared, but did that make it true?

Circle One, Limbo

10. GIORNI

In time, I my guide and I came to the verge of the abyss,
a valley dank and melancholy – oh, that held such thunder
of eternal wails. Obscured, profoundly nebulous it was,
such that although I fixed upon its depths, I failed to
discern any thing within. Still we set off, and my guide
had me make entry to that first circle of the damned.

I found within no tumult, only sighs that trembles made
of the eternal air. The spirits here lacked baptism, instead
of being cast here for their sins upon life; their punishment
was longing without hope.

An elder, toga-clad, did see me pass, and leaped to stand
before me and my guide. "What day?" he cried. "What
day? It comes to fall in two days after that which in its
turn falls one day after the day before yesterday – alas!
My mind is mazed."

So too was mine, my friend, but what of yours?

11. FILOSOFI

We came upon a castle's lovely base, seven times encircled by lofty walls, defended round by a fair rivulet. Within, a meadow full of lush green plants, and people there with solemn eyes and slow, of great authority in countenance; they spoke but seldom, and in gentle tones.

Three stood around in quiet, deep debate, all clearly of the greatest of their kind, and as I saw them wonder came to me. There Socrates, Euclid and Plato stood, and in such worthy company I was naught. But which the very greatest of them all?

"Not I," said Euclid with a gentle smile.
"It is Plato," Socrates declared.
"Socrates is wrong," Plato opined.

"Their modesty forbids," whispered my guide, "but of the three just one is speaking truth."

So who then is the mightiest of the three?

12. SPERICOLATO

On and ever on my guide did press us, on forth from the
quiet, into trembling air, and to a place I came where no
thing shined. A man was there, indignant in his shock.
"He almost ran me down," he said. "The fool! He rode as if
possessed, his horse ablaze. I could not tell his speed, but in
the time it took for him to vanish round the turn, just two
and fifty paces did I walk. In three hundred and twelve of
my steps more, I reached the turn myself, and here we are.
Two leagues an hour is the pace I walk. Such recklessness!"
he mumbled to his beard.

So, from the figures that the man gave up, what is the speed
at which the rider tore?

Circle Two, The Carnal

13. CRUNA D'AGO

The gate past which the second circle lay was guarded by a fearsome judge of all. There Minos stood most horridly, and snarled, examining transgressions at the gate, and he, discriminator of all sins, can see the place in hell for each damned soul.

Before him stood a spirit bold of girth, one much given to self-aggrandizement. "I traded hard," he said. "That much is true. But with that came considerable success. With just two hundred florins did I start, but each new year I had increased my pot by half of what I'd had twelve months before. Eighteen such years straight did I attain, and truly mighty did my wealth become."

"Yet here you are," I said, "facing a judge – one who I would reckon can't be bought – without even a florin still to hand."

What fortune did the spirit leave behind?

14. PIANTO

We came into a place where light was mute, which
bellowed as the sea does in a storm. That hellish hurricane,
which never rests, hurtles the spirits onward in its rage –
whirling them round and smiting, it assails, before it drives
them to the precipice. Oh, then, the shrieks and wailings
and laments!

I learned that those who suffer this torment are damned
because they sinned within the flesh, subjecting reason to
the rule of lust. My guide informed that within one year,
some forty-two per cent of all the men, and twenty-eight
per cent of women too, who died within the mighty walls
of Rome – and found themselves condemned to the dread
pit – had been assigned to stay within this place.

Which year that was, my guide declined to say: but tell
me if you can, with insight true, the ratio of male to
female sin?

15. DEMOCHARES

"Demochares," a spirit moaned, "did live one fourth part of his life aged just a boy, one fifth as youth, one third as man, and then thirteen years as elder afore my death. Demochares, a curse upon your name."

The winds descended, and the spirit quailed, but it helped not, for he was blown away.

Demochares – what age had he attained when that poor wretch was sent to meet his doom?

Circle Three, The Gluttons

16. FRUTTA

In the third circle, wet and cold, gross hail made
from water streaked with filth and gore comes hurtling
down from dull, shadowy skies. The earth receives this
tribute with a stench. Inside, the spirits find themselves
submerged, and turn from side to side in vain attempt
to screen themselves from the eternal ice.

In turning one of them did gaze at me, and at my guide
and master in this place, and called to us in plaintive
disarray: "I had but apples three which, with a peach, did
come to weigh no more than ten ripe plums. That peach
itself did weigh the same as six ripe plums and one lone
apple of its kind. How many plums alone would match
the peach? How many, sirs? I find I can't recall."

17. MIO

"It was for me! Yes, mine it was, all mine!" The soul who
spoke was seized by some distress. "It did belong to me,
and me alone. And yet my kith and kin did use it most,
and rare the day I had it for my use. Not fair, I say, not
fair of them at all."

"Injustice does he claim, but 'tis not so. The situation
he laments is norm. What think you he refers to?" asked
my guide.

18. DOMANDA

Old Cerberus, a monster cruel and vile, with his three throats did bark a constant drone, standing on the souls therein submerged. Red eyes he had, a beard greased and black, and belly large, and hands cruel-armed with claws. He rent the spirits, flayed and quartered them. My guide took up some earth and, fists well filled, he threw it into those rapacious gullets, and stunned the horrid demon in our way.

"The spirits here are often free of sense, or at the least have lost the ways of man," my master did in thoughtful manner muse. "They have forgotten word and gesture both: and yet will some attempt to answer you – at least, to try conveying yea or nay. The trick, of course, is to decipher that, but just one question lone will aid you there. You see the simple truth of what I say, so can you tell me what that question is?"

Circle Four, The Hoarders And Wasters

19. GRANA

Here, I saw people, more than other spots. On one side or the other, with great howls, they rolled weights forward by main force of chest. They clashed together, and then at that point, each one turned backward, rolling in reverse, crying: "Why hoard you?" and "Why squander so?"

"I merely wanted profit!" one fool called, on recognizing us as strangers there. "Two kinds of grain I bought, one fair, one poor. I sold the blend as premium to all. Thirty-two solidi cost the poor – a hundred-weight of grain that is, of course – and forty cost the better: nothing less. The blend I sold at forty-three, no more, and made just twenty-five per cent o'er all. Was that so bad, I ask you, so as to deserve to be caged in here with these fools?"

I thought me that his sin might have involved other factors he had not described. But that is by the by; pray, tell me here, how much of each his grains within his blend?

20. ARDESIAE

Excessive thift, I learned, may be a sin, when love of
wealth does triumph over all, and man forgets his duties
to his Lord. In that dark place a preacher grey I found,
clutching to himself a chest of slates. In broken words,
he told me of the way in which he'd clutched to himself
every bit.

Within his chest he carried here with him the numbered
slates that he had used in life to indicate to those within his
church the numbered hymns for the service there. From
one to eight hundred these hymns ran, and four of them
were called for each day's prayer. The preacher swelled
with pride to let me know that he had just the minimum
of slates required to satisfy each day's new need. He even
bragged how 'six' could serve as 'nine', by simple means
of rotation of slates.

So tell me now, how many slates had he, clutched there to
his bosom in that chest?

Circle Five, The Wrathful And Sullen

21. CATTIVERIA

So we in company with dusky waves – that from a boiling fountain issued forth – made entrance downward by a path uncouth. A marsh this brooklet makes, which is named Styx, and I, who stood intent to behold all, saw people muddied out in that lagoon, all of them naked, with an angry look.

Said my good master: "Son, you now can see beneath the water people there who sigh and make this old swamp bubble at our feet. Wedged in the slime do they lament that they had sullen been while part of life's sweet song."

As we trod round that swamp, a voice came up, and filled with bitter spite and rage it was. "I hate them all, the filthy rutting swine. Oh, Enzo made off with a tavern wench – or was it that Ignacio? I forget. Giano was an orgiast, or could it be that Enzo or old Leo? Ignacio was violence-filled, or was it Giano or Enzo who was so? And Leo was a hashishim for sure – unless that was Ignacio, that is. But, be that as it may, I hate them still!"

Perhaps you can untangle each man's crime?

22. BAGAGLIO

"He made me carry packs," a voice did rage. "The sheer effrontery of that damned boy! A mere four leagues that we did have to go, and what if both my bags were weighted down? So he was young, with uncle past his prime. How so is that my fault? They worked for me! Two bags, two aides: a simple matter, yes? But no; once we set out then naught would do but I be forced to labour, as was 'fair'. Oh, the sheer indignity of it."

For fairness' sake, how long a way did this fool spirit have to carry his own dross?

Circle Six, The Gates Of Dis

23. DIS

"The city drawing near is named as Dis, and holds grave citizens in a great throng." My master's face held naught but kindly calm, and I replied: "Already can I see its mosques and roofs there in the valley deep – all crimson, as if made from flame itself." The city walls appeared to be of iron, and thousands gathered at the gate I saw.

A spirit came to us, all seized by rage. "A third her age, my mother said: a third, before I could be free to seek my way. Well, she was forty-six, and I thirteen. How many years would I have had to wait? There was no choice for me, you understand."

The soul raged on, and left us far behind. I did not seek to learn of what it spoke, but how long would the fool have had to wait?

24. SERRAGLIO

As we approached the gates of that dire place, a strange
and horrid caravan of beasts set out to pass us, driven
on by goads, wielded by teams of herders clad in mauve.
One paused to talk to us, all puffed with pride at the
abominations in his charge. He pointed out to us a pair of
freaks, a four-legged swan and a six-footed sow. The rest,
he claimed, possessed the usual count of legs and feet and
other sundry limbs. Birds and beasts there were within that
throng, though none was blessed with truly wholesome
mien. A count of thirty-six heads did I make, and there
were just one hundred feet in all.

What count therein of birds, and what of beasts?

Circle Six, The Heretics

25. CATENE

A vile stench exuded from that fen which wrapped itself
around the city stern. My eye was drawn towards a far,
high tower, which held aloft a summit flaming red, and in
one moment, on that tower I saw the three infernal Furies,
stained with blood. Megaera, Alecto, Tisiphone; each one
was crowned with serpents, not with hair.

"I came this way before," declared my guide. "Four
prisoners upon my path I found. They were chained
together in a line, kept that way for reasons I don't know.
Their names were written large upon their breasts. Dino
joined to Fons, but did not link to Paolo. Neither was Paolo
so linked to Celio – so then, who was?"

Can you say, my friend, who Celio linked?

26. ERINYES

In fear of Medusa's stony gaze, I turned and looked away
from the Erinyes, in case she came to meet her sisters' call.
Instead a limpid spirit met my sight, pathetic, aye, and
broken-down of mien.

"I knew the man at once on sight, by name." The soul was
clear obsessed with some old wrong. "I had never seen
his face before, nor seen his likeness reproduced from life.
He was not famed, and bore no special marks. He held no
banner that proclaimed his name. And yet despite this all
I knew him there, and let my hatred burn up all my good."

I tried to understand, but I did fail. How did this man so
recognise his foe?

27. ENTRATA

At length, a messenger from heaven came, heavy with disdain for that foul air, and with a wand did open Dis's gates, that we might pass within and on our way. He paused a while to lecture the despised on the folly of their vile arrogance that had given them the thought to bar our path: and then he left, and spoke to us no word, filled as he was with other, deeper cares.

As we passed within, my dear guide looked at me with a visage kind and wise, perceiving as he did my dark distress. "Mysteries on life there are," said he, "so many of them deep and filled with woe. Yet this, I think, is of a lighter cast. Two days before his death, Santino had possessed just five and thirty years of age. Yet when he passed, 'twas plain for all to see that the next year would have seen him thirty-eight. How can this odd situation be?"

Circle Six, The Heretics

28. ANNODATO

We passed into a horrid, spreading plane filled with sepulchres open to the sky. Within, my guide did say, were heretics, those who held false faith or none at all, and those sick tombs were heated in some means. The temperature in them was so vast that flesh would scorch to agony at touch. In some lay hundreds, all crammed in one hole, all burning through and through with dire pain.

"In that tomb," said my guide, "there lies a fool, and with him his disciples, numbered three. They died as one, the three between them with the same year tally that their leader held. The eldest of the three was Flavio. If they'd lived on to such a point as when the ages of the younger two came to total Flavio's, what then would have the age ratio been, between the master then and Flavio at death?

29. CREPUSCOLARE

Within the realm of heresy there lay many men of science so blinded by their arrogance that they'd declared their sure and certain mastery of all life's odd uncertainty. "No soul!" they had declaimed. "No life past death!" – well, none at least for these.

And even still, amongst these proud buffoons were those whose pride did spur them ever on. "Behold," cried one, "Look to the sky and see, when times are right and when the clouds allow, a ray of sunlight streaking from behind a distant mountain or a patch of cloud. Those rays fan out in a majestic way! But there's no need to evoke God in that. The light of our fair Sun is parallel, and all the beams do travel in one line, so how d'you think you come to see such rays? No need for God, I say again!"

No need! How sceptical can one remain in Hell? And yet the question stands – can you explain?

30. CERCHI

We passed amongst the tombs, and as we went, my guide
informed me that in certain ones, the damned had curled
themselves into tight balls – a paroxysm of their pain, he
claimed. I'm sure it made scant difference in the end. But
it gave me thought to wonder this: if packed all tight, and
truly round then what number of souls could contact one
that lay inside the centre of a single layer?

31. PIGRIZIA

Upon the margin of a lofty bank, all made of great rocks
broken in a ring, we came upon a still more cruel throng
– and there, by reason of the horrible excess of stench
the deep abyss throws out, we drew ourselves aside,
behind a tomb.

Before us, there was arguing a wretch, engaged with one
quite similar to he. They had, it seemed, been acquainted
in life. The best that I could understand was this: that
they were called to work within the trade of stone, as
quarrymen of simple means. Ten solidi they earned for
each day's work, but eight solidi was the fine if they
decided it was best to shirk instead. The one had worked
for thirty days for naught, a feat the other could not
comprehend.

My friend, can you speak to the truth of this? How long
did that fool shirk, to earn no pay?

32. VAGHEZZA

"Think not of the smell," declared my guide. "Give yourself time, and you will master it. In place of scent, turn your attention here. A friend of mine in life was somewhat vague, and prone to some surprising lapses there. I asked him once his age, and he replied that he'd forgotten, if you credit that! Instead, he told me of his family. Some twenty years of age his mother was when he was brought forth from her to the world. His brother was two years older than he, his sister four years further older still. He even knew the average age of all the entire group of four of them. Just thirty-nine that was, across them all – and still his own did stay obscure to him."

So how old was my master's vapid friend?

33. BARCA

A final trial my master gave to me to help distract my
mind from that cruel scent that wafted up from deep in
the Abyss. I did remain aware of our dire place, for
noxious though the realms of Hell had been, by far the
worst was saved for those below, the ones most truly
hateful in God's eye.

Two men, he told me, escorting two youths, came upon a
stream that barred their way. A boat there was with which
to get across, but only fit for one man at a time. The youths
could safely make their use of it together, as it were, but
only them. Each man could have no company within. So
what means could they use that all could cross?

Circle Seven (Round One), The Violent Against Neighbours

34. UCCISIONE

The shattered cliff that we had to descend was alpine,
but its ruin was our grace. Without its break there'd have
scarce been a path. Yet, even so, the crack was no kind

sight, and at its mouth, the infamy of Crete stood guard, the horrid Minotaur itself: and when he saw us, it was plain to me that he was one whom anger racks within. My guide goaded the beast to furious rage – much to my discomfort, I must say – and in its frenzy blind we slipped away. Thus we picked our way down that sad incline, and stones did often move beneath my feet. Eventually below us did draw near a river made of boiling blood within which laid those dark fools who injured others.

Within my ken was one who sought the truth, back in the living world so far above. A murder it was given him to solve, and six men had he placed within a manse. Right at the time the murder had occurred, a Valentino was in the kitchen, or the study or conservatory: one room of all those three, that much was sure. Chiatti was in morning room or else in kitchen; Lombardi in turn was found in study, kitchen or in dining room. Bianchi was in the dining room or morning room or kitchen, Stefani in the study, library, conservatory or morning room, and Tomba finally was located in kitchen or the library, or dining room or conservatory.

For sure each man had been alone that time, the murderer inside the morning room. I'll say to you that this is true past doubt: a knowledge of the murderer will show in certainty which room each man was in. So tell me now, which man did do the deed?

35. PIRATERIA

From time to time the dead rose from the blood a little, just to ease their suffering, at which they would draw arrow-fire from guards, mighty centaurs thundering back and forth. One of them I thought I recognized, a savage pirate captain long since hung. Of him 'twas said that he had caught a prince, and made demands of ransom for his life: but also in the ransom was a test, and failure would lead to fates most dire.

A million coins the greedy pirate sought, but brought over the course of ten whole days. The first two days the sum had just to be in excess of one hundred of the coins, the second day at least twice that the first. The next day, though, became somewhat complex; the total brought that dark third day must match the total sum of all the previous days, plus extra that did match the day before. Each day would be the same, and on the tenth, the pirate had to hold his million. No more, no less; the sum must be exact.

Tell me: what did days one and two require?

36. TIRANNO

So that I might escape the river of blood, on which I could not float, unlike my guide – being as I was corporeal man – the centaur Nessus was given to be my steed. With his kind aid I made my way across the boiling gore and the tyrants within: and as we passed, the centaur showed me one – a vile beast he must have been in life. "He slew a family," the centaur said. "Two grandparents, four parents, four children, two parents-in-law, one brother, two sisters, two sons, two daughters, one daughter-in-law and three grandchildren all fell to his blade."

A vile tally, without any doubt, but what's the least headcount he could have claimed?

Circle Seven (Round Two), The Violent Against Themselves

37. NOZZE

Poor Nessus had not reached the other side before we put ourselves within a wood that was not marked by any path at all. No foliage of green in there, just black; the branches gnarled and intertwined, not smooth. Such tangled thickets, dense and filled with thorns, are far beyond even the fiercest beasts. In here did hideous harpies have their nests, and make laments upon the piteous trees.

A voice regaled me from that strange, dark wood, its voice all filled with sadness and with pain. "I am twice as old as my wife was, back when I was as old as she is now. When she would have been as old as I am, together would our ages ninety reach. Instead we ended here, where time is not, and my regret is measured without end."

So how old were the couple so described?

38. AFFRANCATURA

Examining the trees, it came to me – via all the patient teachings of my guide – that these foul things had once been human beings, condemned here for the sin of suicide. I spoke to one sad inmate of this place, and heard from him a tale of foolish woe. His death from poor communications stemmed, and came about not all that long ago.

His land, it seemed, was torn by war, which made the simple act of passing message stern. A full sixth of all missives went astray. So this of course affected them both ways, leading to scant messages in return – and thus much doubt and pain and lack of faith, and in the end departure from the world.

A tragic tale, as most in that wood were: but tell me, if it lies within your grasp, the true percentage chance to get answered.

39. FERRO

"It should have been my time," a soul confessed. "Instead, I failed, and pride condemned me here. A tiny thing it seems from this fell place, but back in life it filled me with such shame. Within my folly, it did seem to me there was no other option left to hand. But tell me now, the truth;

Circle Seven (Round Three), The Violent Against God And Nature

40. DOLORE

The wood behind, we came upon a plain whose very substance every plant denied, which served to stop the forest from its growth. The soil was a thick and arid sand, and weeping souls were clustered all around. And from the sky fell fire, as does snow, meandering to land whereso it will. The sand it touched caught instantly alight, and souls did rush to quench it with their flesh – for best extinguished swiftly is such flame, no matter how much agony it takes. And, at the edge, all racked with flaming pain, there stood before me infamies of old.

Five souls, all broken by their stern travail, locked eternal in a ring of woe. Thus their torment, turned upon itself, driven back and forth upon a web of truth and lie. One man slain, as blameless as a lamb; his killers here entombed for the Minotaur's decree. Yet still they argued guilt and innocence, as if the planning was of no concern, and, of the five, ever two did lie.

At my guide's urging, I heard what each did say; but which had struck the blow I could not tell. Perhaps, my friend, you can see the truth, so tell me – which soul did the awful deed?

Ciro: Felice, you killed that fool.
Lorenzo: He may have; I most certainly did not.
Gaetano: For sure, Pietro is not the one to blame.
Felice: Ciro lies; he does and always has.
Pietro: Perhaps; but then Lorenzo speaks just truth.

41. CAPANEUS

A beastly man all puffed with his disdain lay supine in the sands, defiant still, and claimed to pay no heed to rain of fire. Much filled with arrogance was he in truth, and this in turn tormented him with rage to match the fires burning in his flesh.

"A king he was, who laid foul siege to Thebes." My guide had seen that he had claimed my sight. "In death as well as life he loved to vex, and even made of his bequests a trial. Fifteen hundred gold ducats did he leave to all his kin, arranged in such a way as to ensure that the square root of the sum set for his heir, one half of that left for his second son, two ducats less than the third son's amount, exactly what he left to his old friend, two ducats more than that of the fourth son, two times his daughter's gain, and last of all, the square of his poor wife's meagre bequest, all these sums would yield the same amount. Tell me, if you can, how much each got."

42. CORSE

We followed through that land a rivulet that trickled from the horrid wood of souls and led across the sands towards the edge. Along the way we passed a gibbering soul, his words quite often broken with his pain.

As best as I could tell, it seemed to me that he had made some wager ill-advised. Four men he'd backed to win a certain race, in certain confidence that one would win, for some reason I could never tell. The odds accruing to each of these men were four to one, then five, seven and six to one in kind. The soul had laid his bets so that his total profit for the day would yield him one hundred gold ducats and one besides, given that his stake was not returned. What wagers did he put on that dread race?

43. BESTIAME

Upon that plain I did learn many things, from many souls, all desperate with pain. While some confessed their sins, others held forth about some other memory of theirs, one which they had fixated upon.

One soul recalled a time when drovers met, each man there in charge of some different beasts. Gialli turned to Carfi at that time: "If I did swap six pigs here for your horse, then you would have two times the beasts of me." And Carfi nodded, and to Biani said, "Were I to swap you four cows for your horse, you'd have six times the head count that I had." Biani, lastly, to Gialli turned, and likewise did observe that fourteen sheep for one horse he could swap to leave the latter three times the beasts of he.

No beasts were swapped, but can you tell me here how many animals each man possessed?

44. ONESTA

Three souls we came across, upon that bank, huddled in an acrimonious group. My guide observed that by their mien he knew that each a different quality possessed. In this dread place the import of that news was that one of those souls would always lie, another of them always tell the truth, and that the third of them would either speak.

"I'm not the truthful one," the first declared. "I'm not the liar," stern the second said. "I'm not the one who switches," said the third.

Of these three souls, which one spoke only truth?

45. CERO

"Three candles did I set in a straight line," a hoary, grizzled soul declared to me, "each one set the same distance apart, and each one standing at an even height. The central candle had two times the height of its two brothers standing to each side, but was by far the thinnest of the three. The leftmost one could burn a goodly time; eighteen burning hours was its lot. The central one would last for just four hours and forty-eight minutes when all was told, the rightmost one for nine full hours in truth. I lit them all at once, and later on, when all the three a perfect slope did make, that was the signal for my men to strike. Alas that I was such an utter fool."

How long was it before this came to pass?

Circle Seven (Round Four), The Violent Against Nature And Art

46. APPAIAMENTO

Now in that place reverberation rang, of water falling into the next round. 'Twas like that humming which the beehives make, so deep and dark and sinister that sound. Then shadows three together started forth, running from out a company that passed beneath the rain of burning punishment. In turn they stood before me one by one, and gave to me great cause to think afar.

"This is a curious thing," one said to me, "so that despite my doom it irks me still. For every number, there exists one more which, added or multiplied with the first, will give you the identical result. The only whole such pair is two and two, which either way will bring you up to four, but for the others caught within this link, what is the rule that governs how they form?" I noted that this does not hold for 1.

47. ALBERO

The second told to me a rambling tale about a trip by
boat which ill befell, and all because the vessel rode too
high for it to scrape its mast beneath a bridge. The excess
was not great, the spirit whined, and yet the mast could
not be dropped one inch, and from that sorry fact disaster
fell, and everything which did then flow from it.

It seemed to me right then that in his place, a simple
answer would have come to me regarding how to get
beneath that bridge. My friend, can you say what that
means would be?

48. MUCCHE

The third was most concerned with cows and grass, and
calculating pasturage required. It seemed to me an odd
fixation here, where naught did rain but fire, and no thing
grew, but many are the ways man comes to sin, and varied
the regrets amongst the damned.

Three cows, the soul did state, could so survive on two
acres of pasture for two weeks. That same space for four
weeks two cows could feed. It is important here that I
make note that grass did grow all times during its use,
and all this growth was likewise counted up. The question
that bedevilled this soul so was, given six acres, and six
long weeks, how many cows could he have safely fed?

Circle Seven (Round Three), The Violent Against Art

49. GERYON

"Behold the monster with the pointed tail, who shatters hills and breaks both walls and swords. Behold the filth who infects all the world."

This much to me my Guide began to say, when that unclean old image of deceit came up and thrust its head and chest ashore. Its face was that of a benign old man, but as a lion its chest and front paws were, complete with a most horrid, hairy mane. Foul wings of leather sprang from on its back, past which its trunk was like that of a snake, dwindling behind it to near-naught, save the venomed scorpion-like tip.

Upon this horrid vision we must ride, so that we could descend into the pit. My mind, engaged in recoil from that thought, decided to return to happier times, and muse over another trip I'd known.

Three of us there were, and just one horse, which could take just one man as extra to its usual rider – who was our third. The distance that we had before us then was forty weary leagues, no less nor more. Two leagues an hour was the pace I walked, my friend just one, but then our rider eight. We felt in fairness that we should arrive in synchrony at our final end point. Our rider aided us as much he could, reducing to a minimum our walks and thus the time that the whole journey took, no matter that he rode thus back and forth. We took a uniform pace each throughout according to the rates I shared before. So say, my friend, how long did this all take, before we did arrive at our end spot?

50. PAVESE

When I had to my destination come along with my two
friends who'd come with me, our dear host engaged us in a
game. The four of us a coloured band did take, one red, one
blue, one green and one plain white. My memory of which
was which is hazed; perhaps you can assist me in
this plight?

The way that I remember it is thus: my walking friend,
the slowcoach, was not red, and likewise did he not select
the green. My riding friend was neither green nor white.
Our Host did not pick white or red himself, and I myself
was neither green nor red. One other thing do I remember
clear: that if the Walker did not choose the white, then by
no means did Rider select red. But of this all, what colour
then was I?

51. EREDITA

Later on that trip our host explained that he had found
an epitaph most quaint, one that he had no way to well
explain, and asked us how there could be such a thing.
According to that queer engraving, within one tomb
of just six people lay two grandmothers with their two
granddaughters, two husbands settled with their two
wives dear, two fathers with their two dear daughters
sweet, two mothers with their two sons always true,
two maidens with their mothers stern but fair, and
two sisters with their elder brothers dear.

How could such a strange pass have come to be?

Circle Eight (Bolgia One), The Panderers And Seducers

52. MUNIFICENZA

There is a place in Hell called Malebolge, wholly of stone and of an iron hue, as is the circle that around it turns. Right in the middle of that place malign there yawns an abyss vilely deep and wide, which I will tell you of in its due course. Round, then, is the space which thus remains 'twixt pit below and towering cliff above, and ten distinct, sour valleys does it hold. The Bolgia of Malebolge are these, the home of fraudulent, malicious souls, and to this place was I with my guide brought, upon the wretched back of Geryon.

No sooner were we there than one fell soul attempted to ingratiate with us by telling of the monies he disbursed to various dependents he had known. A monetary sum each week did he split up amongst the applicants thereto, each one receiving an exact same share. One week, he told us, he had to declare five fewer applicants would sure result in each share being two solidi more. Instead of that, the actual tally was such that four more persons hung upon his tails, and so the share was one solidus less. How much did he give away each week?

53. FLAGELLI

Along the bottom of this valley's moat – for so the many
Bolgia were arranged – were naked sinners harried to and
fro by mighty demons wielding scourges cruel. Three such
sinners found themselves by us, and I was minded to learn
of their fates when Virgil – he my guide – reminded me
that some amongst them were still prone to lie. And so I
asked them if they spake the truth.

The first, with mouth agape, did nod his head. The second
turned around and said to me, "He claims that he will tell
you only truth." The third one frowned, and in hectoring
tone pointed to the first and just said "Liar!". Which of
them, if any, could I trust?

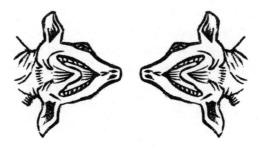

Circle Eight (Bolgia Two), The Flatterers

54. LUSINGA

From there to the next Bolgia we crossed, a vile crevice deeper than our sight, so that we had to climb upon a bridge, and reach its arch to look into the moat. In that sick place were sinners without end, smothered in the filth of mankind's ordure, to such point as to be beyond all ken. In here were those manipulators dire who had with flatteries destroyed and sown the seeds of further harsh downfall – and now they reaped the just rewards of this.

One poor fool was still so basely made that our presence did enliven him to try to fill some urge to flatter us, by appealing to the prowess of our minds. "A simple matter, gentlemen," he said, "one that will prove momentary for you. I can see by your noble cut of brow that nothing which I ask will confound you. Two glasses, please, just see within your minds, each made for wine, but one just half the size. The smaller one I fill half-way with wine, the larger to the mark of just one third. I then fill both with water, by the by, and then combine both in an empty vase. You see, of course, what my question will be – what is the true proportion now of wine?"

55. UCCELLI

Our sewage-dwelling fool was not yet done. "See, 'twas simplicity itself for you. I mark superiority on sight. Allow me, please, to prove my judgment true. So tell me this: three chickens and one duck were sold for the same price as just two geese. Three geese, two ducks and one lone chicken brought their vendor twenty-five bright solidi. What then was the price of each of these, when considered as just one fowl alone? Each one was priced in some whole solidi."

We left him there attempting us to charm, and went with some relief upon our way, but what do you make for his answer there?

Circle Eight (Bolgia Three), The Simoniacs

56. MAGUS

Oh, Simon Magus and his disciples, those vile fools who things of God do sell, here found themselves down in the depths of hell. In this third Bolgia, the livid stone was filled with perforations of one size, each circular, and smaller than a font. Within in each hole a wretch was planted down, so that he was covered to mid-thigh, and fire all the exposed flesh did burn, causing each one deep and torrid pain. So God in all his justice deigns to deal with those who prostitute spiritual oath.

One we found had died upon a day – November the eleventh, by your ken; such age had he attained that he had lived as long in the tenth century as he had lived in the eleventh, bearing that it was in 1128 he died. What, then, was his day and date of birth?

57. INGANNO

We passed these procurers of the divine, moving on
our way through this dread place, and although each was
writhing in dread pain, there still was one who boasted
of misdeed. "I was born in March," the fool declared, "yet
celebrate my day of birth in June, and in the February of
my last year, I married my own mother – it is true! And
all of this without one word of lie."

It seemed my noble guide was unimpressed for, after all,
to this dark fate he'd come. But, my friend, I wonder; can
you say if there's a way his boast could yet be true?

Circle Eight (Bolgia Four), The Fortune-Tellers

58. TIRESIAS

On to that fourth Bolgia we trod, and so I peered down into the depths, and bathed they were in tears of agony. Silent and weeping here were the damned, and wondrously each one distorted was, from chin to the beginning of the chest. Towards the rear their countenances turned, so that they must walk backwards to advance, and forward sight had been denied to them.

One of them was chosen by my guide, who knew him for some certain infamy. In verbal intercourse did we engage, and quickly did I come to see the mien whose horrid stamp had cast him to this place. Two people did he tell me of, whom he had possessed some sure knowledge of in life. Forty-four years the difference in their age; the product of those ages one thousand, two hundred and eighty years in full. What age did each one of the two attain?

59. DISSOLUTEZZA

Then he with whom we spoke began to wail and beat himself in signs of sure distress, but when the fit of pain had lifted off, he told us of his kin-folk from his time. No more than eighty nor no less than fifty years of age had he attained upon his death. Each of his sons, he claimed, had had as many sons as brothers when he'd died. What's more, the tally of his years of age was equal that sum of sons and grandsons both. How old was the profligate when he had died?

60. FORZA

With clarity, he fixed me with his eye, this soul whose face above his buttocks stood, and bold declared that he the body knew so well so as to be able to say which motion was most powerful of all. With no machine or lever or other aid, which is the strongest movement that there is?

Circle Eight (Bolgia Five), The Grafters

61. MALACODA

And so to the next valley did we come, where all to see was just a tarry mass that seethed and boiled and spat its clamminess, and naught there was save bubbles in the pitch. Then as I watched a demon raced along, a cowering soul well clutched within its grasp, and flung the sinner deep into the tar head-first, with force to drive him out of sight. Then, spying us, the demon and his friends – how barbarous they seemed, all dark as night, with craggy wings and claws and wicked teeth – made clamour, so that my guide thrust me back, and forward stepped to meet their chosen one. Malacoda was the demon's name, and he agreed to put Virgil to trial, with prize safe passage deeper into hell.

There was a table, Malacoda claimed, so perfect smooth and frictionless and huge that those who found themselves at rest on it would be unable to move back or forth. Only up or down could these souls move, not left nor right nor to nor fro at all. Every such attempt would come to naught, and nowhere was an edge for them to clasp. How then could the table be escaped?

62. SCREZIO

Next Malacoda told us of a game, a simple matter
decided just by chance, where each participant had equal
hope. This game was played in series of fifteen, to add to
both the interest and length. The winner was the one who
took most games, and to him alone did all the prize accrue.

So far, so good, but this was just the base. Two demons
played, and had gone ten games in when by no fault their
play had then to cease. The score did stand at six round
games to four, but there was much dispute on how to settle.
The leader claimed that all the prize was his. The other said
the prize should equal split. Neither of these modes was
truly fair. How would you have settled the dispute?

63. OVINI

Last, Malacoda spoke to us of sheep. Four brothers did he conjure from his mind, and each one had a certain flock of sheep. Cristo's sheep outmatched Drago's by ten, and if said Cristo were to give a fourth of all his sheep to Bruno, then 'twas so that Arlo and Cristo's flocks, counted as one, would match the ones that Bruno and Drago held. Then leading on from that, if Arlo in turn gave one third of his sheep to Bruno's flock, and Bruno passed a fourth of that to Cristo, who in turn then gave one fifth his flock to Drago, and last of all Bruno once more did give one quarter of the sheep that he possessed, to be divided equally amongst the other three, then they would all have the same size of flock.

With all that said and done, the task was clear. How many sheep did each of them possess?

64. COLLEGAMENTI

So thus were given we free pass to roam, and Malacoda
warned us of the path ahead which had been shattered
long years hence. Instead he bade us venture with his men,
who went to check the sinners did not stir, and took a
different path that we could use to venture on our way to
further in.

Said one, called Barbariccia, "I fain recall a long and
winding chain of souls that trudged round and around
at doleful pace. I think it was elsewhere in Malebolge.
I wondered me how long that train did stretch, and
knowing that I walked a yard each pace, I decided that I
would find out. So first I walked along that sorry rank,
keeping to a constant pace, of course, moving in the
direction that they trod, and one hundred and forty steps
I took. Then I turned around and walked on back, going
as it were against the flow, and only twenty steps of mine
sufficed to bring me to the end of that sad load. Sir poet,
you are counted with the wise, or so it seems to this one,
here and now, so tell me if you can, how long the chain?"

65. DANNAZIONE

"I have a clutch of souls within my care," did Barbariccia proudly declare. "My business has been very good of late, and in my stretch the numbers have well grown. Last year, my care was just 250 souls, a mix of male and female, of course. I have been extra diligent since then. Today I have eight times as many there, and thrice as fast the females have grown. Despise me not; it is God's work I do, dispensing the just punishments he metes."

That gave me pause for thought. I wonder now, with how many of each sex did he then start?

66. DIVERSIVO

Soon chaos did erupt upon the shore, where certain souls
sought to avoid the pain of being boiled eternally in pitch,
and thus did cluster at the liquid's edge. And while his men
flew off to sort the mess, and put the fear of God back in
the damned, dread Barbariccia did pause, and share with
us one final puzzle he had gleaned.

"Take all the numbers one to nine, save six, which is to be
omitted from your line, and pick from them two groups of
figures four. These are to be arranged into two sums, which
come to total the self-same amount. You may reorder digits
as you please, and count adjacent ones as numbers whole – to
make, say, twenty-three or forty-nine – but integers alone
may you construct. Can you meet this challenge I decree?"

Circle Eight (Bolgia Six), The Hypocrites

67. FRATELLI

In that next ditch, a painted people there we found, who walked with footsteps very slow, a-weeping, tired and vanquished as they were. They had on cloaks with cowls, the hoods low down before their eyes, and fashioned in that way that monks' robes are. So gilded were these robes that they did shine, a spectre of magnificence indeed, but inside they were heavier than lead, a hot, exhausting burden for each step.

"Oh, how I labour now!" cried one sad soul. "I never did a stroke of work in life, but still condemned my sons for laziness, particularly the youngest, poor Pascal. A tradesman I, and my sons were my tools. Emilio and Fausto could, the pair of them, prepare a shipment full in just eight days, that it were ready for the Duke. Emilio and Pascal paired together instead would take a ninth day for the job, and Fausto and Pascal required a tenth."

A fool, for sure, but I do wonder now, how long would poor Pascal require alone?

68. ALIENAZIONE

Within that grim and weary trench a group of souls
engaged in rancour did I see. Approaching them, an
argument came clear that left them free to shift some blame
around, and so it led to squabbling and ire. But my guide
and Master pointed out that none of them was truthful to
the core; instead each one did stick by statements three,
and of those three was always one a lie.

Said One, "It was not me. I have never
destroyed anything. Four did it."

Said Two, "I did not do it. This is Hell!
Five is not my friend."

Said Three, "I am innocent. I do not
know Five. Four is guilty."

Said Four, "I am not guilty. Five is the
one. One lied about me."

Said Five, "I am innocent. Two is guilty.
I have known Three for years."

Which of the souls was guilty of this thing?

69. CAMARGUE

Within that place was one tormented soul who had been of his crushing mantle stripped, and he was fastened nude across the path, that all his fellows walk upon him must. That wretch was crucified into his place with cruel stakes that pinned him to the ground.

He told us of the way ahead, and more, of those famed steeds of the Camargue, those herds whose members are all snowy white. It's true that the white horses are a sight, and that they used to run in varied herds which ran the spectrum of a horse's tone, but over time only the white remained. My friend, can you shed light upon this piece, and say how such a breed could come to pass?

Circle Eight (Bolgia Seven), The Thieves

70. COLONNATO

A horrid place, that seventh Bolgia was, such that
remembrance of it chills my blood. A deep, dark valley, all
aswarm with such monstrous serpents of fell kind that I could
scarcely credit such sights in front of me. Within this place,
a truly dismal throng of sinners, running naked and affright,
fled to and hither from the hideous snakes. Each one had hands
most cruelly pulled behind them which were locked in place
by serpents dire, all knotted as they were around the wrists.

"I robbed my master," one confessed to me. "He caught me in
the very act itself. I was just property, you see, a slave, and so
he chose the punishment I'd get. He had me walk in Diana's
temple, all up and down the columns that were there. Some
seven columns stood in that stark row, and glorious in purity
they were. Thus starting at the top, he bade me walk and count
along each column as I went, to turn round at each end and
head right back, accounting sixth as eighth and on and on,
so that my count was interrupted not. A thousand columns
had I to mark out, and tell him which the thousandth of
them was. But he of course, the great Pythagoras, already
knew the one where I should fall."

Could you have made the same deduction, friend?

84

71. FUGGIASCO

A panicked wretch who fled across our sight, pursued
by some old serpent of cruel mien, did stumble in his
everlasting flight. As swift as arrows, that vile snake did
leap and seize itself upon the damned one's neck. It
wrapped itself around once and again, and suddenly the
soul was wreathed in flame. In moments did he char and
burn away to nothing more than ash upon the plain, a
process which occasioned agony. Those ashes then did
slowly coalesce back into the visage we had just seen,
and painful too was this, 'twas plain to see.

"A thief I was," the phoenix soul explained. "Captured,
I did plan a great escape. My cell was down a corridor of
doors, five of them including mine, which did open now
and then on their own times. When all five of the doors did
open up at once, that was the time when my cruel guard did
check to ensure I was still in place. This happened slightly
less than twice each hour. The nearest door to me did open
up exactly every hundred and five seconds; the second every
one minute and ten seconds; the third in two minutes and
fifty-five; and finally the last each thirty-five seconds, no
more and yet no less. To sprint from one to next would take
more time than each door remained open, there's no doubt
– twenty seconds long such dash would claim. Two minutes
and a half was all the time that I could spend out of my cell
without alarm, the sound of which would cause all doors to
lock. The trick, of course, was then to figure out how long
the time between the guard's clear sight and the moment
when I must first flee my cell. It mattered not, of course,
for here I am. Repentance would have been a better friend."

72. MILITI

The tale of the thief reminded me of an event I'd known another time when a small squad of troops had to deploy in such a way as time was most precise, but with all haste 'twas possible to glean. The distance to dispatch was twenty leagues. A fellow with a carriage they thus found, who said his trap could cover twenty leagues in just one hour, but it could only hold four men at once, and they were twelve in all. He bade them walk, knowing that they all were well-trained so as to march four leagues an hour. He would take four men part of the way and leave them thus to march unto the end, return then for a second batch of four, and then a third, to drive unto the end, so that all twelve would reach there as one man. How long a time then did this journey take?

73. TRONCHI

Screaming his defiance to God and me, the thief was
wrapped round and around with snakes. One coiled around
his neck and bound his voice, and round his arms another,
and rebound him, clinching itself together so, in front,
that with them he could not a motion make.

In his division thus he minded me of some encounter
early in my life in which I'd seen a man divide a tree into a
heap of sorry scraps of log. The wood he'd bundled up into
ten heaps, each one consisting there of twenty pounds, with
not a scrap of timber left behind. He had a mighty scale to
aid this feat, complete with massive panniers of brass, but
weights to measure with he had just two, and these were
fifty pounds, and ninety too, hardly best suited to the heaps
he sought. Yet did he divide the wood with ease, taking just
nine weighings overall. How did he accomplish such
a thing?

74. ONELLI

A Centaur lumbered past us in that place, all filled with anger and with bitter wrath, and he was truly carpeted with snakes, most clearly agonized for all his sins. Cacus was his name, my Master said, responsible for fraudulent thefts made from the great herd which he had near to him. It was Hercules who sent him to his fate – one that he did so richly deserve.

From that great herd, three different types of beast he took and burdened with his loads; each kind was given over to a certain task. Such tasks divided, what we know is this: if donkeys carried wine, horses took oil;while if donkeys carried oil, the mules took wine. If horses took the wine, the mules held oil. From this, is there one breed whose load we know?

75. METAMORFOSI

After a time, three sinners found us there, watching that dread Centaur as he ran. They approached us when, most suddenly, there leapt out of the dark a serpent dire, with six cruel clawéd feet along its length. It sprang upon one of the three souls there, and wrapped itself around him from behind. Its claws dug into him and clasped him tight, so he was held completely in its clutch. His arms and legs and belly held its feet, and then it sank its teeth in both his cheeks. Then, just as if their substance was warm wax, the two began to mix and meld their forms, so neither seemed what he had been before. Their two heads were already joined in one, into one face where two had been dissolved, two intermingled shapes bearing scant form. All that dark while he screamed and howled with pain. It was enough to make a Titan blanch.

"Alas, Agnello," one of the others said. "We were in life third cousins once removed – upon my mother's side, that is to say. Yet even now, in this fell place, I find one ancient lingering curiosity that will not flee in spite of this horror. What relation was his grandmother to my son?"

Circle Eight (Bolgia Eight), The Evil Counsellors

76. LUCCIOLE

In taking leave of that vile snake-filled pit, we clambered out and to another vale, a place of darkness that was lit throughout by tiny flecks of flame as glow-worms seem. As we got close to that Stygian ditch, obvious it became that each bright glow was nothing less than a damned soul aflame, consumed eternal with the fire of God.

At this, my Master told me what I saw – 'twas those who'd given counsel malicious, and doing so led others from their path, and all in cause of puffing their own name, or filling up their coffers with pure gold.

A quad of souls entwined I then espied, a veteran who with machinations dark had caught three generations of his kin, and tied them into sharing his wild fate. The soldier and his great-grandson combined, their ages at their deaths exactly matched the ages of his son and grandson summed. The soldier's age, if its digits were reversed, would give the age on death of his own son. Likewise did this odd relationship extend to his grandson and great-grandson. Each one's age a number prime did match – can you then tell me how old each one was?

77. D'AZZARDO

Another flaming soul that spun on past had convinced
fools of the verity of dream. A game of chance the victim
had foreseen, and in this game the fellow had resolved to
wager sums at six to one, and six to one again, and then
at thirty-six to one, and last, at just eighteen to one, and
from these stakes – which would not be returned, no matter
what – one of the four wagers would come to pass, and he
would become significantly richer, profiting as he would
for certainty two hundred and ten golden ducats. Nothing
of the sort did come to pass, and the poor fool was lost to
poverty, all his worldly riches squandered thus. But what
sum would each stake have had to be, to guarantee than
when all stakes were paid, two hundred and ten ducats
he had gained?

Circle Eight (Bolgia Eight), The Evil Counsellors

78. UOVA

Then in the valley lit by those corpse-flames we came upon a conflagration grand, encompassing, as it did have to do, a soul who'd been a true bull of a man. Although through tongue of fire he did speak, which gave his voice a conflagration's tone, still did he sound out loud and resonant, as if he were a truly blesséd man. Despite his pain and anguish, this great wight did still purport to offer thoughts to hand, and put to me a trio of delights to vex the mind of any greater one.

The first he claimed was simple beyond worth, but I admit I did not find it so. If it can be honestly declared that one and a half hens will lay one and a half eggs in just one and a half days when all is said and done, then, still of hens, how many and a half, which lay better by half, will lay half a score and a half again, in a week and a half?

79. PARENTELA

The second question that the blaze did pose regarded a small family in life. A lady of the Bartolini line had several children whom she doted on.

When there were just three boys – Aldo, Nico, Ludo were they called – that formed her line, their combined ages summed to half of hers. When five years had passed since that time, a sister Alia had then been born, and all four children's ages summed as one were equal then in total to their mother. A further ten years on, and Guilia had joined her siblings as a final child. The eldest, Aldo, was himself as old as Ludo and Alia combined. The children all together in one mass were twice the age of their kind mother dear. Her age was that of her first two children, and Aldo's matched the age of the two girls.

From all that tangle, can you find the way to tell the age of each at that last time?

80. IMBARDATA

Then, finally, the soul did put to me a matter that concerned those hardy folks who chose to make a life on the high seas. It's clear to me that for a nautical pursuit, a hardy stomach is a boon, but our hotly flaming companion said – through shrieks and wails of agony, of course – that it were possible, with cunning strong, to fashion wagon wheels that in their turn would mimic the high seas in their rough chop.

Can you see how this feat might be achieved? (I make no question of its value here!)

Circle Eight (Bolgia Nine), The Sowers Of Discord

81. BRIGADIERI

Approaching the next ditch, in there I saw the most
hideous morass of vile wounds. The damned who to that
valley were condemned were those who had divided men
on earth, and for their crimes they here now were split.
No barrel, rent by centre-piece or spur, was ever shattered
so as one I saw, split from the chin right down the torso
bold. Beneath his legs were dangling entrails grim; his
heart was visible, and that messy sack which turns all
eaten food to nasty waste. He looked at me and pulled
apart his breast, and cried out: "See how I do rend me up."

So do division's teachers meet their fate, those who would
through counsel worlds divide. In such a dire place are
many souls who did engage in matters clerical, and
politicians likewise; soldiers too – all of those cruel
professionals of strife.

An army just o'er twenty-one thousand men was led by
brigadiers five. It was known that of its five brigades, the
same headcount of men was to be found in one third of
the First, two sevenths of the Second, seven twelfths of
the third, nine thirteenths of the fourth, and fifteen
twenty-secondths of the fifth. How many men were
there in each brigade?

82. INDOVINELLO

A different means of division then came to me, and did
remind me of a time when I had taken tutelage, for so
little can divide all the folk of earth as leaving some
deprived of learning time. In this Bolgia, I felt quite
sure, would be those who had denied lessons to some.

My tutor had called my attention once to an odd
mathematical conceit. The digits one to nine he had
displayed, and told me to make use of each one once in
arranging a pair of sums in the form that A+B equalled
X+Y. The digits could be coupled into pairs that marked a
larger number, say fourteen, and even into vulgar fractions
set, but that's the outer bound of their abuse.

My friend, can you see how this thing is done?

83. LASCITO

Amongst the cleft in twain I found a pair of brothers whose mendacity, it seemed, had landed them in this cruel place where they could reap the benefits of their mean ways. Their father on his death had made bequest to both of them, according to his will. Eight thousand, two hundred and thirty-five was the value of his wealth in solidi. The younger brother had a certain share, the rest to go direct to the elder. Within the will the sum was clearly marked: 1647 over 8235.

Finding the will, one brother did attempt to alter that marked share in his favour, and using some careful sanding of ink, removed one digit from both top and base. Imagine his surprise when then he saw that the proportion of wealth remained unchanged. So, greatly daring and driven by greed, he performed the same nasty feat again – and once again, the sum remained the same. In fury he did try one final time, but once again it was to no avail.

In what order did he the digits bleach?

Circle Eight (Bolgia Ten), The Falsifiers

84. CRIVELLARE

In climbing the next barrier to me, and crossing to the last of Malebolge's dread valleys, that one nearest the abyss, I felt a strange lament, like arrows barbed with pity and, at this, I had to place my hands across my ears lest I be struck. If all the sick of Rome were gathered up and mustered to assemble in one ditch, then still it would be less than I found here. Such a stench rose up, and a clamour too, that I quailed to see, in that valley dark great scattered heaps of falsifiers brought down to be as like the worm brought down to crawl, manifest with the sickness in their souls.

And in that horrid dark a voice called forth a dirge, a riddle known to men of old.

> He who holds it does confess it not.
> He who takes it does so ignorant.
> He who knows it does refuse its touch.
> And still, alas, bold men do die for it.

Dear one, pray tell me, what this warns against.

85. COMPLEANNI

So there, within that writhing mass of flesh, all wracked with pained disease and torment just, there languished those who had pretended arts unnatural; their goal, as always is, was nothing more than just base gain of gold.

My Master turned to me with jaundiced eye, and spoke of things those wretches did pretend in life, and still maintained beyond that vale, when all vain hope had fled for ever more.

A heap he indicated, then one more, and others, that were scattered all around, and each did hold a measure of the damned. "They put great stock in day and month of birth, as tools to pry the foolish from their coin, and so they lie before us here and now. A certain number of them in one group suffices to ensure – one time in two – a pair of them had the same date of birth. Pray tell me, poet, what size group is that?"

86. SORELLE

All sorts of flimflam alchemists convey, the better to part
unwary folk from gold. Such eccentricities oft involve
age, and birth, and matters parallel to those. One of the
writhing carriers of plague who grovelled at our feet
amongst the muck erupted out with such a blinding
spiel that you would scarcely credit it made sense.

"Two sisters do I know," the sinner called. "Chiara and
Aida are they named. Counted together, they are forty-four.
Chiara is possessed of twice the age that Aida had when
Chiara was half as old as Aida will be when Aida is three
times as old as Chiara was when she, Chiara, was three
time the age of Aida."

We stared a moment long at that old fraud, and then we
went away, but can you see how old each of the sisters
has to be?

87. PROFUMO

Great Virgil did explain to me a trick that those within this Bolgia oft prized, impressive as it was to people mild, who lacked the same experience they held. The import of the trick, as he explained, lay in the famous stern recalcitrance of glass-wrought perfume bottles to give up the stoppers, glass, that sealed up their necks. Brute force is not the answer, he explained, for it and accident walk hand in hand.

But knowing as you do about the world, perhaps you can divine the trick's import.

88. LOTTATORE

As we passed along that sordid pit, all pestilential with the fruit of sin, we did approach the heart of the abyss. It was a thought that did not gladden hearts – what fool would long to plumb the depths of Hell – but it did seem this was to be my task, and I resolved to do my best in this.

Yet as we walked, that horrid voice rang out which I had
heard just a short time before, and honestly my heart
within me shrank, so that I felt the urge to be long gone.
"Fear not," my guide declared. "Recall your place; this is
the haunt of those whose trade is fraud. Dire though the
wretched voice may be, there is no power in him to cause
you harm." Emboldened thus, I listened to his words.

> "Christ the Lord, the bringer of all delight,
> Created me for combat. When my Lord,
> Did send me forth to fight, his foes I scorched.
> I oft approach the Earth, and without touch,
> Afflict whole hosts of your humanity;
> At times, though, I do gladden hearts of men,
> And then console those whom I fought before.
> They feel my kindness, they who felt my ire
> When, after suffering, I soothe their lives."

Can you decode the import of this verse?

89. FAMIGLIE

As we approached the Titans of the pit, who guard the central heart of Malebolge, my guide was well aware my spirits sank, and gave my mind some better grist to mull. A family he told me of in turn, one I suspect he conjured from whole cloth: but that is by the by; it did its task.

A man and wife did have just children three, Donata, Cinzia and Rosalie. The difference in age 'twixt man and wife was equal to the gaps that did exist between Donata and then Rosalie, and also Rosalie and Cinzia. The ages of sister Donata and Cinzia multiplied together came to match the age of the father, no less. Likewise did the ages of Donata and Rosalie together multiplied just equal their mother's. Added together, all those varied ages amount to exactly ninety years; 'tis most precise. What, then, was the age of each of them?

Circle Eight (Central Pit), The Giants

90. AVARO

We turned our backs on that disease-soaked ditch, and
headed to the edge of Malebolge. Within that place 'twas
neither night or day, but some embroiled shadowy pastiche,
a turbulent, foul twilight of its kind. My sight thus reached
a little in advance, and many lofty towers I seemed to see,
and also hear the blare of a loud horn so deafening as to
make thunder faint. I did ask my guide "What city, that?"
and, asking, was transported to my youth, where I had
known a street as tenebrous with storied towers rising
through the mist.

A miser whom I had heard men tell of did live on that
dark and bespattered lane. A goodly sum of cash had
he attained, which he maintained in three assorted coin –
gold ducats, silver florins and solidi. Of each the number
same did he possess. He kept his wealth distributed in
bags, and each one held the same amount of each of the
three types of coin that he possessed. Within this rule, he
regularly changed the number of such bags that he did use
– sometimes six, or eight, or seven too; even four or three
from time to time.

I wondered then, and wonder still today, what is the
smallest sum he could have held?

91. CAPRI

Beholding my expression then, my guide gave me a kind and understanding look and told me of a truth I'd not have guessed. "Know that these are not towers but giants," he said, "and they are in the well, around the bank, from navel downward buried, all of them." Impossible it seemed to me, yet true it obviously was, so my mind reeled. I was reminded of the strange, dark death of Georgio Grimaldi of Capri. He died on January the fourteenth, and was duly buried to eternal rest a full two days beforehand, on the twelfth of that same month in that same year. No hint of cruel malice was involved, so tell me, friend, how did this come to be?

Circle Nine (Round One), The Treacherous To Kin

92. TESTAMENTO

In passing then vast Nimrod and his kin, that huge progenitor of babble dire, we came to giant Antaeus, and he was left to have some movement to his arm. At the earnest urging of my wise guide, the Titan lifted us up in his hand and swiftly lowered us down to the base of Hell itself where Satan dwells, that horrid circle known as Cocytus.

In front of me there stretched a plain of ice, as deep and thick as no winter has known, and down within it, locked inside its grip, were here and there and everywhere dread souls, from neck below imprisoned in the cold. And in this place of kin who had harmed kin, Caina in the gazetteer of Hell, there was naught but crushing, icy pain, an agony beyond the ken of all. Yet still the damned entombed in ice spoke up, and begged of me to tread upon them not, lest my steps extra suffering did bring.

One of the damned described to me a will, a testament that had produced much strife, and led to his incarceration here. The testator had, earlier in life, produced a will that matched his fortune large, and did account exactly for each coin. His eldest child was to receive the sum of one thousand solidi exact, and also to be added on to that, one third of the estate that then remained. The second child would get two thousand as a base amount, and then again a third of what was left on top, and so progressing thus down to the final child who would find that the geometric base amount was exact, with none left over from which to take a third. Some time later, closer to his death, when he had birthed two further children dear – and improved his fortunes by some lot – he did rewrite his will the self-same way, again resulting in amounts exact.

How much was each child due from each bequest?

93. CUGINI

"My cousin did me harm, or so I thought." The soul who spoke out thus looked most folorn. "Three businesses of mine were cruelly robbed across the space of just one short weekend. There, people saw a most distinctive man, all sun-kissed, tall and muscular besides, and with a beaky nose and bushy beard. Suspicion on my cousin duly fell, for though he was clean-shaven when we called, it is no matter to remove a beard, and in all other ways he fit the bill. He also, by the by, knew of my works, and where each of my workshops could be found. I took the matter into my own hand, and finished off his miserable life. Alas! It was not he who'd done the deed, and had I acted with a cooler head, his innocence was plain for all to see."

A cooler head indeed did he have now, but to what clear sign does he refer?

Circle Nine (Round Two), The Treacherous To Country

94. SPIAGGIA

In crossing to the second of the rounds of Cocytus,
I saw no change between Caina and Antenora's spread;
the endless fields of ice ran on unchanged. Yet here were
those who had betrayed their lands. I accidentally kicked
one in the head, but had I his identity before, I am not sure
that I'd have stayed my foot. As we thus passed, I thought
about warm sands, which seemed to be so distant from us
now. I did recall that walking on a beach, along the line
where the water has fled, each step one takes does change
the sand so that it briefly turns all pale and dry again. And
yet one fact in this I know for sure: that sand does never
function as a sponge. It cannot be you've squeezed the
liquid out. So what, I wonder, causes this effect?

95. FIAMME

"That soul" – my guide did point one out to me – "is known to me for many reasons dark. He married in the year 1101, and his widow left the earth a few months shy of 1140, poor woman."

"How so, oh mighty Virgil?" did I ask.

"She suffered much," said he. "But listen here. The man's age when he died was one nineteenth the value of the year of his grim birth. How old was he when he met his end?"

Circle Nine (Round Three), The Treacherous To Guest And Host

96. AVENA

In Ptolomea, the third of the rounds, the sinners in the ice were flattened out and laid upon their backs to gaze upwards, so that their cheeks would lock in tear-fed ice. Their very weeping there won't let them weep, so grief that finds a barrier of their eyes turns inwards to increase their agony. One soul revealed that those within this place do often come here long before their death, for once the soul has earned its place herein, foul demons do arrive to cart it hence, and stay within the flesh in that soul's stead, wreaking such vile havoc as they may.

A horrid Genoese regaled me with some complex tale of sin, and murder and abandonment and such, but I confess my mind did not remain to give to him the attention he craved. I saw no reason why he should deserve even cool comfort after his sick sins. So what I took from his long tale was this: a mule there was, a donkey and a horse; and feeds there were just two, of oats or hay. If the mule ate oats, the donkey got exactly the same feed as did the horse, and if the donkey made a meal of oats, the mule ate that feed which the horse did not. Then finally, when the horse ate of hay, the mule ate the same feed as the donkey. Which animal always ate the same feed?

97. BOTTIGLIA

"I contrived a point of honour," wept one soul. "My host
had in his cellar five fine wines of various impressive
vintage years. Demanding that in deference to my age he
must provide me with two bottles of wine whose ages
paired did match my sum of years, I knowingly did set him
up to fail. He tried, and did obtain nine different sums when
adding all ten possibilities – in order twenty, twenty-four,
thirty, then thirty-five and thirty-six, forty and forty-one,
and forty-five and, last, to fifty-one, and that was all of it.
My age, however, none of these years matched, and so I
claimed offence and ran him through, and used his wife
and daughters as I would."

A vile act, and fit the punishment. But tell me here, what
ages were those wines?

Circle Nine (Round Four), The Treacherous To Their Masters

98. FINESTRINI

So last of all to Judecca we came, its name taken from
Judas of ill fame, in which there lay all those whose

treachery was to their rightful masters so disposed. The greatest of the infamous lay here, so fully covered over by the ice of Cocytus, and so aligned within, that they were cast like straws within a wind. Some did lie flat, whilst others stood erect, one on his feet, another on his head. Still more were bent and twisted in the ice, contorted into shapes most pitiful.

Sweet Virgil there did put then unto me a tutelary parable of sorts, one whose true meaning would come clear in time, and later still the lesson that he sought. "A window, square," said he, "and one foot high, when split into four equal panes by frame, will yield four shafts of light, and of each one, it will measure half a foot on every side." Enthusiastically did I agree that this did seem most certain to be true. "So tell me then," my gentle guide did say. "Another window, again with four sides, each one again to be a foot in length, but split this time by frame into eight parts, each part again with all sides equal length. It can be done, but you must divine how."

Pray tell, dear friend, what is the truth of this?

99. STRAGI

My guide did bid me pause upon the ice, all heedless of
the horrid gales of air that blew so chill throughout this
part of Hell, and gestured to a region to our left. "Within
that part of Judecca, there are a particular collection
of damned. Their infamy is vast but, even more, they
each have killed the same number of men, through their
peregrinations, while in life. Incredible though the tally
seems, the total of the lives that they have claimed comes
to one million, and one hundred and eleven thousand and
one hundred and eleven – and their common tally is more
than their sum. How many of the damned do suffer there?"

Far, far too many, it would seem to me, but yet I held my
tongue in that dread place. Can you, my friend, discover
that grim sum?

The Heart Of Hell

100. LUCIFER

The Emperor of the kingdom of the damned was from mid-chest below entombed in ice, and closer to the giants did I compare than did their mightiest seem to his arms. That something could exist of such a size! He had been fair once, as he now was foul. Oh, what a marvel it appeared to me, when I saw there three faces on his head, melted together above each shoulder, and each of them a thing of horror clear. The central one was red, the right-hand pale, the left of them was swarthy, and beneath this trio loathsome wings did sprout, alas, like unto those of some poor, leprous bat. Those horrid things did ever wave and beat, and from that air was Cocytus congealed. Upon a soul each vile mouth did chew, and ever rend and rip and shred and tear. Vile Judas found his doom in that red maw, while Brutus hung in horror from the left and Cassius, still stoic, from the right.

So then we moved to flee that dreadful place, by climbing through the hair of the Great Beast, and downward we descended out of Hell, and I was well delivered from my travail. But as we climbed, the enemy did speak his words most vexedly into my mind, a voice of horror and of thunder both. "Ten statements will I tell you, little fool. Your task is to determine truth from lie. Prepare yourself, for they will come but once." I drew a breath; there was naught else to do.

"At least one of these statements is a lie;
At least two of these ten statements are false;
At least three of these ten statements untrue;
At least four of these ten statements are false;
At least five of these ten statements are lies;
At least six of these ten statements are false;
At least seven of these statements are lies;
At least eight of these ten statements are false;
At least nine of these ten statements untrue;
All ten of these my statements are plain lies."

I will confess, this riddle haunts me still.

Solutions

1. FONTANA
If '5' is worth 4, then '$1\frac{0}{3}$', or '3 $\frac{1}{3}$', is worth 2 $\frac{2}{3}$.

2. SACCHETTO
If all the labels are wrong, just one investigation need be made. Assume the sacks are A, B and C. If you open sack A and find contents B*, then the sack labelled B will hold C*, and the sack labelled C will hold A*. If sack B held A*, then C would have to hold its proper contents, breaking the rule of each one being mislabelled.

3. VIRGIL
The first shade is the honest one. Both shades must answer "Yes" to the question of whether they are honest; the truthful one because it is truth, and the liar because it is a lie: but only the honest one is able to say that the other will reply "Yes", for that is truth for both of them. The liar will have to lie, and claim that the other will say "No."

4. SEGARE
Gathering 3 $\frac{1}{13}$th heaps will take $\frac{8}{13}$ths of an hour, and processing that amount will take $\frac{5}{13}$ths of an hour, giving a total of 1 hour.

5. RETAGGIO
The two sums are 24 and 76 florins. One third of 24 is 8, which when subtracted from 19, one quarter of 76, produces 11.

6. FEDELTA

His wife had just given birth to their baby.

7. PREDATORE

Yes. After 55 seconds, the hound will overtake the fowl, having run about 968 feet.

8. AGGRUPPAMENTO

Such flexibility requires geometric procession as far as possible. So combining 1, 2, 4, 8, 16, 32, 64, 128, 256 and 489 – all that remains when the previous amounts have been removed – will allow you to reach any amount from 1 to 1000.

9. CHARON

Anna is indeed the best overall weaver of the three. For rapidity, Anna to Carla is 5:2, and Anna to Maria is 3:4 – or 20:15:6 for Maria, Anna and Carla in order. Lightness gives Maria 5:1 over Anna and 3:5 to Carla, or 15:3:25 in the same order as lightness. Warmth tells us that Carla's scarves are four times as good as Maria's, and Anna's are three times as good again, so the ratio is 3.75:60:15 in order, standardised to 15 for the girl in common. Totalling those scores, we get 38.75 for Maria, 78 for Anna and 46 for Carla.

10. GIORNI
Tomorrow.

11. FILOSOFI
Socrates and Plato cannot both be lying, so one of them is telling the truth. That means Euclid is lying. The only consistent option is that Euclid is the greatest, and Plato is telling the truth.

12. SPERICOLATO
The rider travels 312+52=364 paces while the man walks 52, so the rider is going 364/52=7 times the speed of the man, or 14 leagues an hour.

13. CRUNA D'AGO
Compounding eighteen years of 50 per cent increase, starting from 200 florins, yields a net fortune of 295578.38 florins.

14. PIANTO
42 to 28 represents a ratio of 3:2.

15. DEMOCHARES

60. $\frac{1}{3}x + \frac{1}{4}x + \frac{1}{5}x + 13 = x$, so $\frac{47}{60}x + 13 = x$, or x=60.

16. FRUTTA

Seven plums. Combining the two, six plums and an apple, and three apples, matches ten plums. So plums and apples weigh the same.

17. MIO

The thing that is yours, and yours alone, which others get to use more than you do is your name.

18. DOMANDA

Any question with an answer that has to be yes – such as "Are we in Hell?"

19. GRANA

If 43 solidi is a 25 per cent profit, then the price of the mix must be 34.4 solidi, which means it is 70 per cent poor grain and 30 per cent fair grain.

20. ARDESIAE

82. Consider the worst case for each number. For 1, it would be number 111 plus three others with two 1s in -- nine slates. For 0 and 8 there is no possible triple, so just eight slates will do, and while no nines are needed, four numbers consisting entirely of 6s and 9s is possible, so there have to be twelve 6s. $8+9+9+9+9+9+12+9+8+0=82$. You could, of course, extend all the way to 999 with just one extra '8' slate.

21. CATTIVERIA

Enzo ran off with the tavern wench, Giano was violent, Ignacio was the hashishim, and Leo was the orgiast.

22. BAGAGLIO

Two bags to go four leagues means eight leagues' worth of load over three people, or $2 \frac{2}{3}$ leagues each, ideally split into three sessions of $1 \frac{1}{3}$ league for the first bag, the second bag, and being unladen.

23. DIS

$3 \frac{1}{2}$ years. $\frac{46}{13} = 3.53$, but we need the age to divide three times exactly. $\frac{47}{13} = 3.36$, which is closer; progress on, and you'll find that $\frac{49.5}{16.5} = 3$.

24. SERRAGLIO

Allowing for the two freaks adding four legs more than usual, 24 birds and 12 beasts.

25. CATENE

Dino.

26. ERINYES

The pair were identical twins, separated at birth.

27. ENTRATA

Santino died on January 1, the day after his birthday. Two days before, he was 35. One day before, he was 36. On January 1, it was the start of a new year that would see his 37th birthday; the year after would have held his 38th birthday.

28. ANNODATO

It would be 1:2. At death, we know $a + b + F = L$.
Later, $a+t + b+t = F+t$, or $a + b - F = t$;
also $a + b + F + t = L + t$.

29. CREPUSCOLARE

It's an optical illusion: just a trick of perspective. The shaft of light is a straight beam all the way up, but without visual clues to make it plain, it's very easy to see it as fanning out from a source.

30. CERCHI

Assuming equal sizes, you can pack six circular shapes around one central one.

31. PIGRIZIA

Working for $13\frac{1}{3}$ days would earn the same amount as shirking for $16\frac{2}{3}$ days would cost in fines.

32. VAGHEZZA

The age of Virgil's friend must be 32 (which leaves his brother as 34, his sister as 38 and his mother as 52).

33. BARCA

The two youths cross. One returns. One man crosses. The other youth returns. Again, the two youths cross, one returns, the second man crosses and the second youth returns. Finally, the two youths cross one last time to join their elders.

34. UCCISIONE

Stefani. If Bianchi is the murderer, all we can know is that Chiatti is in the kitchen. If Chiatti is the murderer, we can deduce nothing at all. So it has to be Stefani, which places Tomba in the library, Bianchi in the dining room, Valentino in the conservatory, Chiatti in the kitchen and Lombardi in the study.

35. PIRATERIA

144 and 298. Calculate the sums to be paid in total by considering the days as a set of exponentially growing equations: #1: x, #2: y, #3: x + 2y, #4: 3x + 5y, #5: 8x + 13y, #6: 21x + 34y, #7: 55x + 89y, #8:144x + 233y, #9: 377x + 610y,and #10: 987x + 1597y. These sum to 1597x + 2584y = 1000000.

36. TIRANNO

The smallest number that fits the bill is seven – a married couple, their three children (two female and one male) and the husband's parents.

37. NOZZE

The husband is 40, the wife 30. When he was 30, she was 20; when she was 40, he would have been 50.

38. AFFRANCATURA

5 out of 6 messages will arrive, and of those, 5 out of 6 replies will arrive. So the chance is 25/36, or 69.4 per cent.

39. FERRO

The hole will keep its same proportions within the disc, so, yes, it will get bigger.

40. DOLORE
Pietro; Ciro and Gaetano are the liars.

41. CAPANEUS
The common sum is 36, and the bequests are 1,296, 72, 38, 36, 34, 18 and 6.

42. CORSE
The wagers are 105, 84, 70 and 60 ducats. We know that $4a = 5b = 6c = 7d = a+b+c+d+101 = x$. So x has to have 4, 5, 6, and 7 as factors. From that we can quite easily find $x=420$.

43. BESTIAME
Gialli has 11 pigs, Carfi has 7 cows and Biani has 21 sheep.

44. ONESTA
The third. Neither the truthful nor lying souls can deny being truthful -- the former because it's a lie, the latter because it's true -- so the first soul is the one who changes. The second one could be either truthful or lying, but for the third soul, the liar again would not be able to deny being the changer, so that must be the truthful soul, and the second one is the liar.

45. CERO

3 hours. The left-hand candle will have lost $\frac{1}{6}$ of its height, the right-most $\frac{1}{3}$, and the central one $\frac{5}{8}$, which is equivalent to half its height (to bring it to the same starting height as the other two) plus a further quarter. So the candles then effectively have $\frac{5}{6}$, $\frac{3}{4}$ and $\frac{2}{3}$ of one side-candle left. Convert to 12ths, and you see that $\frac{10}{12}$, $\frac{9}{12}$ and $\frac{8}{12}$ form a perfect slope.

46. APPAIAMENTO

The number which you can add to or multiply a starting number by to get the same total both times is a fraction of the form 1 1/(n) where (n) is 1 less than your starting number. So the pairs are 3 and 1 1/2, 4 and 1/3, and so on.

47. ALBERO

You can lower the mast by taking on some extra weight -- most easily by allowing a small amount of water into the boat so that it sits lower.

48. MUCCHE

Three cows take two acres and four acre-weeks of growth over two weeks. Two cows take two acres and eight acre-weeks of growth over four weeks. By considering these two conditions, we can see that one acre of standing pasture is equalled by four weeks of growth, and a cow needs the equivalent of half of an acre of pasture per week. Six acres will gain the equivalent of nine acres over six weeks, for an equivalent of fifteen acres of pasture. That would mean 30 cows for one week – or 5 cows for 6 weeks.

49. GERYON

10 hours and 7.31 minutes. To maximise progress, the slower walker must be carried first, and dropped off approximately 5.85 leagues from the end, after 4.27 hours. By the time the rider has got back to him, slightly over 2.5 hours later, Dante will have walked 13.66 leagues over 6.83 hours, leaving 26.34 leagues to go.

50. PAVESE

From the statements, Rider must be red, and thus Host must be green. Rider being red means Walker must be white, which leaves Dante as blue.

51. EREDITA

Two widows with adult sons each marry the son of the other, and each new couple produces a daughter, resulting in six individuals who fulfil all the requirements listed.

52. MUNIFICENZA

120 solidi. Twenty applications would each get 6 solidi. Five less, fifteen, would get 8 each; four more, 24, would each get 5.

53. FLAGELLI

Either the first or the third is lying, and there's no way to tell which. However, the second is making an undeniable statement of truth, so he can be trusted.

54. LUSINGA

The large glass contributes a third of wine, and two thirds water. The smaller contributes an effective quarter-glass of wine and quarter-glass of water. Therefore we have a third plus a quarter of wine, and two thirds plus a quarter of water -- or seven eighteenths of wine to eleven eighteenths of water.

55. UCCELLI

Substitute out the equations and standardise for one fowl, and you'll find for an exact number of solidi, chicken cost 2, ducks 4 and geese 5.

56. MAGUS

February 19, 1073, remembering that the year 1100 was not a leap year.

57. INGANNO

The man was born during the month of June in a place named March. Becoming a priest, he officiated at his mother's marriage in the February before his death. Presumably she had been widowed.

58. TIRESIAS

Their ages were 64 and 20.

59. DISSOLUTEZZA

Sixty-four, with eight sons, each one having seven sons (and brothers) of his own, for a total of 56 grandsons.

60. FORZA

Lifting your heels up to stand on the ball of your foot. The calf muscles are the most powerful and efficient in the human body.

61. MALACODA

In the absence of a steady stream of possessions to throw, you could escape the table by exhaling. When you inhale, air comes from every angle around your mouth, and exerts very little force, but when you exhale, the blast is focused, particularly if you blow firmly. Thus you could slide yourself off the table with just your breath, similar to rocket propulsion or a toy pop-pop boat.

62. SCREZIO

The fair option, since it is pure chance, is to work out how likely it is that each demon will be the winner, and then divide the pot on that basis. There are five games left to play. The leader must win two of them; the other needs to win four. There are 32 possible outcomes of five 50/50 matches in a row, and only six of those involve the second-place demon winning four or five games. So he has a 6/32 chance of winning, and the leader has a 26/32 chance. Rounding to the nearest whole number, the prize should thus be divided as 81 per cent to the leader and 19 per cent to the other.

63. OVINI

There are 180 sheep in total, with the even distribution at the end coming to 45 sheep, so Arlo has 60, Bruno 50, Cristo 40 and Drago 30.

64. COLLEGAMENTI

35 yards. Going forward, assuming the chain is of length 'a', and for each yard the demon walks, the souls shuffle forwards 'b', then $a + 140b = 140$. Similarly, on the way back, $a - 20b = 20$. Therefore b must be one quarter of a yard, and a is 35 yards.

65. DANNAZIONE

If x is female and y is male, then originally $x + y = 250$. Allowing for the increase of males as z, then also $x + 3zx + y + zy = 2000$. The increase factor z is 5, leading to an increase of 1000 male souls and 750 female souls, meaning that the distribution now is 800 female and 1200 male. Therefore Barbariccia started with 50 female souls and 200 male souls.

66. DIVERSIVO

$85+92 = 173+4$ (which $= 177$).

67. FRATELLI

22 days. The tallies we have are averages of work-rate, spread across two men, so $(E+F)/4=8$, $(E+P)/4=9$ and $(F+P)/4=10$. Multiply out, and we have $E+F=32$, $E+P=36$ and $F+P=40$. Solve for P, so that $P=40-F$, and substitute into the other P equation, so that $E+40-F=36$, or $F=E+4$, then $E+E+4=32$, or $E=14$, so $F=18$ and $P=22$.

68. ALIENAZIONE

Four says that he is innocent, and that One's accusation is false. He can only tell one lie, so both those have to be truth and he and Five are not guilty. One and Three both accuse Four – a lie – and declare innocence, so they are not guilty. Therefore Two is the guilty one.

69. CAMARGUE

A strong environmental pressure against non-white horses had to be in play. Specifically, the cause was a particular breed of horseflies in the early Camargue area. These flies had a very strong preference for attacking darker horses, and they caused severe debilitation. They tended to leave white horses alone, however – some sort of issue with perception, possibly – so that over time, only white ones remained.

70. COLONNATO

The end point is the 4th column. In each back and forth

of counting, the central columns are counted twice, and the end columns just once. So, in this case, one full circuit is 12 columns. Divide the total distance – 1000 – by 12. The quotient of the division is the number of full circuits to walk, in this case 83, and the remainder is the column to finish at in that circuit. In this case, it's 4, but if it had been more than 7, then you'd just need to count back along the line the required distance – so 8 would be the sixth column, 9 the fifth, and so on.

71. FUGGIASCO

The thief has to leave at 19 mins and 15 seconds. The doors all open on a multiple of 35 seconds – 3x, 2x, 5x, 4x and 1x. The prisoner cannot make use of simultaneous opening, so needs the five doors to open on successive beats. That will mean he's out for just 4x35s = 2 mins 20, less than the alarm time. The guard appears every sixty beats, the lowest common multiple of 2, 3, 4, and 5. The final door opens every beat, so to find the escape point, we need a series of four sequential numbers between 0 and 60 divisible by 3, 2, 5 and 4 in that order. The only possibility is 33, 34, 35, 36 (and 37). So the prisoner must leave 33x35 =1155 seconds, or 19.25 minutes, after the guard's last check.

72. MILITI

In an hour, the coach can take four men twelve miles ahead and then come back eight, to the four-mile mark. In the same time, the remaining men can walk to that same mark. Picking up a second load of men, the coachman does the same, going forward twelve miles, dropping the men at the 16-mile point (which their friends have now reached), and going back to the eight-mile point to meet the last four at the end of the second hour. Finally, he heads straight to the finish, a 12-mile haul which takes 12/20ths of an hour. So the total time is 2h 36mins.

73. TRONCHI

With the 50lb and 90lb weights in the two pans, you can measure a heap of 40lbs. Do this four times, and your full 200lbs of wood is divided up into five stacks. Each stack can then be split between the two unweighted pans so that it balances, taking five more measurements.

74. ONELLI

The horses always carry oil. The horses cannot carry wine if the donkeys do, and so take oil; but if the donkeys take oil, the mules take wine, and if the horses take wine the mules must have oil instead. So therefore, if the donkeys take oil, the horses still must do so.

75. METAMORFOSI

Agnello's grandmother was second cousin twice removed to the other soul's son.

76. LUCCIOLE

97 + 13 = 79 + 31; 97 flips to 79 and 31 to 13, and all four are prime.

77. D'AZZARDO

The longest odds are 36 to 1. Aiming to win a total prize of 360 ducats means 10 at 36:1, 20 at 18:1, and two lots of 60 at 6:1. That's a total stake of 150 ducats, and 360 - 150 = 210.

78. UOVA

One half, technically. If 1.5 hens lays 1.5 eggs in 1.5 days, then 1 hen lays 1 egg in 1.5 days. A single "better hen by half" will lay 1 egg in 0.75 days. That's 4 eggs in three days, 8 in 6, 12 in 9, and 15 (half a score and half again = 10+5) in 10.5 days (1.5 weeks). One half plus a half is one whole hen.

79. PARENTELA
The answer can only be that Signora Bartolini is 39, Aldo is 21, Nico and Ludo are twins at 18, Alia is 12 and Giulia is 9.

80. IMBARDATA
Oval wheels will make a land vehicle pitch back and forth. If the lateral alignment of these oval wheels is against each other rather than with each other, the vehicle will also roll left and right.

81. BRIGADIERI
Start with the common denominator of the fractions, which is 12012, and represent all the fractions with that. Then factor your top numbers together and divide through to get the minimum possible amounts that each brigade could hold – 1890, 2205, 1080, 910 and 924 respectively. Together, they come to just over 7000, but the army is a little over 21000, so multiple by three for the correct totals; 5670, 6615, 3240, 2730 and 2772, and the common sum of each fraction is 1890.

82. INDOVINELLO
The simplest solution is 79 + 5 1/3 = 84 + 2/6.

83. LASCITO

The only possible solution is that starting from $^{1647}/_{8235}$, he rubbed out $^4/_2$ to give $^{167}/_{835}$, then $^6/_3$ to give $^{17}/_{85}$, and finally $^7/_8$ to give $^1/_5$.

84. CRIVELLARE

Counterfeit money.

85. COMPLEANNI

23 people ensures a 50.7% chance that two members of the group will share the same birthday. There's a 364/365 chance that any two people will have different birthdays. To calculate the chance of everyone in the group having a different birthday, you have to consider each member of the group in turn as a separate probability. So go through the group one by one. The first person definitely has a different birthday to everyone who has gone before -- because no-one has gone before -- which is a chance of 365/365. The second person, as above, has a 364/365 chance of having a different birthday. The third person now has two dates to rule out, so has a 363/365 chance of being different. Each person's chance of having a unique birthday decreases linearly. To find the chance of every person having a different birthday, multiply all the separate chances together. So for 23 people to all have different birthdays, (365*364*363*...*343) / (365^23) = 49.3%; or, in other words, a 50.7% that at least two people have the same birthday. By the time you get to 50 people, the chance is 97%, and it's 99% at 57 people, but, of course, it's not 100% until you get to 366 people.

86. SORELLE

When Chiara was three times as old as Aida, Chiara was 16½ and Aida 5½ (11 years younger). Then we get 49½ for the age Aida will be when she is three times as old as Chiara was then. When Chiara was half this she was 24¾. And at that time Aida must have been 13¾ (11 years younger). Or, in the other direction, Chiara is (27½) twice as old as Aida was (13¾) when Chiara was half as old (24¾) as Aida will be (49½) when Aida is three times as old (49½) as Chiara was (16½) when Chiara was (16½) three times as old as Aida (5½).

So the age of Chiara to that of Aida must be in the proportion 5 to 3, and as the sum of their ages is 44, Chiara is 27½ and Aida 16½.

87. PROFUMO

You need to heat the neck of the bottle without heating the stopper, so that the glass expands to free it. The way to do this is to wrap a narrow strip of cloth around the neck of the bottle and pull it back and forth rapidly. The friction will generate heat, and allow the stopper to be withdrawn. A more general method of heating, such as holding it under a hot tap, will not work, since both bottle and stopper, being both glass, will expand at the same rate.

88. LOTTATORE

The sun.

89. FAMIGLIE

The children are all the same age – triplets – and the parents are the same age as each other. The three kids are aged 6, and the parents are both 36.

90. AVARO

168 each of ducats, florins and solidi.

91. CAPRI

He was trapped underground by a collapse or cave-in, beyond reach or recovery, and died two days later.

92. TESTAMENTO

This problem can be solved by starting with the youngest child – who has to get X thousand solidi exactly – and working back. You know that the next-oldest child will get (X-1) thousand solidi, plus half of the previous bequests, so on up to the first. You also know that the total has to come out to a whole number of solidi. Simple trial will show that 4 and 6 children are the solution. In the first will, that means shares (from youngest to oldest) of 4000, 5000, 6500 and 8750, from a total bequest of 24250 solidi; in the second will, shares of 6000, 8000, 11000, 15500, 22250 and 32375 from a total of 95125 solidi.

93. CUGINI

The cousin, like the thief, was tanned. It takes months to grow a big beard, during which time the skin of the face is shielded from the sun. If he had shaved a beard off so recently, his mouth and neck would be several shades lighter than the rest of his face.

94. SPIAGGIA

Your weight displaces sand from beneath your foot. In order to accommodate you, surrounding sand is forced to rise up. Being now above the water level, the sand drains out, becoming dry. It then slowly draws water back up by capillary action, so the effect only last a few seconds.

95. FIAMME

If his age at death is x, then the date of death is 19x+x years, or 20x. Between 1101 and 1139, only 1120 is divisible by 20. 1120/20 = 56, his age, and he was born in 1064.

96. AVENA

The only non-contradictory answer is that the mule always eats hay.

97. BOTTIGLIA

Each bottle will be compared to four other bottles in its ten possibilities. That means the total of all pairs must divide by four. The total of the nine pairs given is 322, and the missing tenth pair is the same as one of the nine. One of those nine added to 322 must give a result divisible by 4, and that one is 30, with 352/4 being 88, the sum of the five ages. The smallest pair is 20, and the largest 51, so we know there's no overlap between those two. Subtract both from 88 to find the middle wine is aged 17 years. Plug that into the second-smallest weighing to find a second age (24-17 = 7) and into the second-largest to find a third (45-17 = 28); and then turn back to the minimum and maximum to find (20-7 = 13) and (51-28 = 23). The ages of the wines are 7, 13, 17, 23 and 28 years.

98. FINESTRINI

The window must be diamond-shaped, and the eight parts equilateral triangles rather than squares, and then you will find that it can be achieved.

99. STRAGI

The number 1111111 only has two factors – 239 and 4649. Therefore 239 souls are each responsible for the deaths of 4649 victims.

100. LUCIFER

The first five statements are true, the other five false.
The rule in problems of this sort is that so long as there
are an even number of statements, half are true, the
other half false. All other options become self-inconsistent.
Odd numbers of statements have no valid logical solution.

PICTURE CREDITS

The publishers would like to thank the following sources for their kind
permission to reproduce the pictures in this book.

AKG-Images: 30, 54, 74

Author collection: 7, 8, 11, 15, 18, 29, 59, 85, 117

The Bridgeman Art Library: 21

iStockphoto.com: 12, 24, 27, 35, 38, 39, 43, 49, 54, 63, 67, 70, 71, 79, 83,
87, 95, 100, 104, 111, 115, 119

Every effort has been made to acknowledge correctly and contact the
source and or copyright holder of each picture and Carlton Books
Limited apologises for any unintentional errors or omissions, which
will be corrected in future editions of this book.